The Anxiety First Aid Kit

Matthew Petchinsky

The Anxiety First Aid Kit

The Anxiety First Aid Kit: Quick Tools to Calm Your Mind
By: Matthew Petchinsky

I am like you, I suffer from severe anxiety is why I have created this book, thank you.

-Matthew Petchinsky

Introduction: The Calm Within the Storm

Anxiety is a universal human experience—one that connects us all, no matter our background, profession, or stage in life. At its core, anxiety is the body's way of signaling that something demands attention or action, a mechanism designed to protect and prepare us. Yet, in today's fast-paced, highly demanding world, this natural response can become overwhelming, persistent, and debilitating. For many, anxiety feels less like a helpful tool and more like a storm they're caught in, unable to find shelter.

But here's the good news: anxiety can be managed. You don't have to stay stuck in the storm. You can find calm even when chaos surrounds you. Like a well-stocked first aid kit for physical injuries, this book is your *Anxiety First Aid Kit*—a practical and actionable resource designed to help you navigate moments of high stress, calm your mind, and build long-term resilience.

Why This Book?

This book was created with one primary goal: to empower you to take control of your anxiety. Whether you're facing a sudden panic attack, chronic worry, or general unease, *The Anxiety First Aid Kit* offers immediate tools to help you regain your footing.

However, the book goes beyond temporary fixes. Anxiety isn't just about managing the moment—it's about understanding your mind, your body, and how they interact. By combining quick-relief techniques with foundational strategies, you'll not only survive the storm but learn to prevent future tempests from taking over your life.

A Practical Guide for Every Need

Life doesn't wait for you to sit down and read a 500-page textbook on managing anxiety, and neither does this book. Every tool, exercise, and technique in this book is intentionally designed to be simple, accessible, and adaptable to your unique needs. You don't need a degree in psychology or hours of free time to benefit from the insights here.

Here's what you can expect:

1. **Immediate Relief Tools**

   When anxiety strikes, you need something fast and effective. From breathing exercises to grounding techniques, this book equips you with methods to calm your mind and body within minutes.

2. **Building Resilience for the Long Term**

   Beyond short-term fixes, this book helps you create a sustainable mental health plan. You'll learn how to challenge anxious thoughts, improve physical health, and develop a more balanced and resilient mindset.

3. **A Personalized Approach**

   Anxiety looks different for everyone. This book empowers you to create your own "first aid kit" by selecting the tools that resonate most with you. It's not about following a rigid formula—it's about finding what works for you.

How to Use This Book

There's no one right way to approach this book. It's designed to meet you wherever you are in your journey. Whether you're looking for immediate relief, long-term strategies, or a combination of both, this guide adapts to your needs. Here's how to make the most of it:

- **Read It Cover-to-Cover**

  If you want a comprehensive understanding of anxiety and how to manage it, start at Chapter 1 and read sequentially. Each chapter builds on the last, offering a complete toolkit for anxiety relief.

- **Skip to What You Need**

  If you're experiencing acute anxiety and need quick relief, jump directly to Chapter 2. If you're curious about building a resilient mindset, start with Chapter 3. Use the table of contents to find the sections that address your immediate concerns.

- **Revisit and Adapt**

  Anxiety isn't a one-size-fits-all experience, and neither is this book. As you grow and your needs evolve, come back to these chapters. Try new tools, refine old ones, and continue building your personalized first aid kit.

What's Inside the Kit

This book is divided into five actionable chapters, each focusing on a critical aspect of anxiety management:

1. **Understanding Anxiety—The Mind-Body Connection**
   Gain a foundational understanding of how anxiety works and why your body reacts the way it does. Knowledge is power, and this chapter sets the stage for effective management.

2. **Quick Calming Techniques for Immediate Relief**
   Discover simple exercises and tools to stop anxiety in its tracks. These methods are designed to be fast, effective, and easy to implement anywhere.

3. **Building a Resilient Mindset**
   Learn how to shift your thinking patterns, challenge anxious thoughts, and cultivate mindfulness practices that keep anxiety at bay.

4. **Physical Tools to Manage Anxiety**
   Explore how exercise, nutrition, and sleep play a vital role in calming your mind and strengthening your body's ability to cope with stress.

5. **Creating Your Personal Anxiety First Aid Kit**
   This final chapter helps you assemble your own customized toolkit, filled with techniques, tools, and strategies tailored to your needs.

You'll also find two appendices packed with resources, worksheets, and additional tips to deepen your understanding and practice.

You Are Not Alone

Managing anxiety can feel isolating, but you're not alone. By picking up this book, you've already taken a powerful step toward regaining control. The tools you'll find here are meant to guide you through the moments when anxiety feels overwhelming and equip you for a future where you face challenges with confidence and calm.

So take a deep breath, turn the page, and let's begin this journey to-gether. The storm may be raging now, but with the right tools, you'll find your calm within it.

Chapter 1: Understanding Anxiety—The Mind-Body Connection

Anxiety is a term that's often used casually—"I'm anxious about this meeting," or "I feel anxious when I drive." But what is anxiety really, and how is it different from everyday stress? To understand how to manage it, we must first break it down to its core components: its definition, its effects on the mind and body, and the role it plays in our lives. This chapter will give you a clear understanding of anxiety, setting the foundation for practical strategies to manage it.

What Is Anxiety, and How Is It Different from Stress?

Anxiety and stress are closely related, but they are not the same.

- **Stress** is a response to an external trigger, such as a tight deadline, an argument, or a life event like moving or losing a job. Stress tends to dissipate once the external situation resolves. It's your body's way of preparing you to face a challenge—think of it as a short-term alarm system.
- **Anxiety**, on the other hand, often persists even in the absence of an identifiable external trigger. It is more internal and can arise from fears, worries, or thoughts about the future. Unlike stress, anxiety can linger and intensify, affecting not only your emotions but also your physical health.

In essence, stress tends to be situational and temporary, whereas anxiety is more pervasive and can become a chronic condition if left unchecked.

The Physiological and Psychological Components of Anxiety

Anxiety is not "just in your head." It's a deeply rooted mind-body experience, involving intricate interactions between your thoughts, emotions, and physical state.

The Physiological Components of Anxiety

When you experience anxiety, your body reacts in noticeable ways:

1. **Racing Heartbeat (Tachycardia):** Your heart pumps faster to circulate blood to vital organs, preparing your body for action.
2. **Rapid Breathing (Hyperventilation):** Your breathing quickens to increase oxygen intake, but this can sometimes lead to dizziness or a feeling of breathlessness.
3. **Tensed Muscles:** Your muscles tighten, often leading to aches, headaches, or stiffness.
4. **Sweating:** Your body activates sweat glands as part of its preparation to cool down from exertion, even if no physical activity occurs.
5. **Digestive Issues:** Anxiety can disrupt digestion, causing nausea, stomachaches, or an uneasy feeling in your gut.

The Psychological Components of Anxiety

Anxiety also manifests mentally, creating a whirlwind of thoughts and emotions:

1. **Overthinking and Rumination:** A cycle of repetitive, often negative thoughts that seem impossible to stop.
2. **Fear and Dread:** Persistent feelings of apprehension or worry, often without a clear cause.
3. **Irritability or Restlessness:** A constant feeling of being on edge, unable to relax.
4. **Difficulty Concentrating:** Anxiety often clouds focus, making it hard to think clearly or make decisions.

These physical and psychological responses work together, often creating a feedback loop—physical symptoms intensify mental distress, and mental distress exacerbates physical symptoms.

The "Fight-or-Flight" Response: Anxiety's Biological Foundation

Anxiety is rooted in one of the oldest survival mechanisms of the human body: the **fight-or-flight response**. This response evolved to protect us from threats, enabling us to either confront danger (fight) or escape it (flight).

How It Works

When your brain perceives a threat—real or imagined—it sends an alarm signal to the amygdala, the part of your brain responsible for processing emotions. The amygdala then activates the hypothalamus, which triggers a cascade of physiological changes:

- Your adrenal glands release adrenaline and cortisol, stress hormones that prepare your body for action.
- Blood flow is redirected from non-essential functions, like digestion, to essential ones, like muscles and the brain.
- Your senses become heightened, ready to detect and respond to danger.

When It Becomes a Problem

The fight-or-flight response is critical for survival in dangerous situations. However, in modern life, this system is often triggered unnecessarily—by worries about work, relationships, or even thoughts of "what if." This constant activation can lead to chronic anxiety, as the brain and body remain in a heightened state of alert, even when no real danger is present.

Short-Term vs. Long-Term Anxiety Management

Understanding the difference between short-term and long-term approaches to anxiety management is crucial for developing an effective strategy.

Short-Term Management: Addressing the Immediate Storm

Short-term management focuses on techniques to quickly reduce anxiety when it strikes. These strategies include:

- Breathing exercises to calm your nervous system.
- Grounding techniques to anchor yourself in the present moment.
- Physical movement, like walking or stretching, to release pent-up energy.

These tools are like the bandages and antiseptics in a first aid kit—they don't fix the underlying cause of anxiety but provide immediate relief.

Long-Term Management: Building a Resilient Foundation

Long-term strategies aim to address the root causes of anxiety and reduce its frequency and intensity over time. These approaches include:

- **Cognitive Behavioral Therapy (CBT):** A structured way of identifying and changing negative thought patterns.
- **Mindfulness Practices:** Regular meditation or mindfulness exercises to train your brain to stay present.
- **Lifestyle Adjustments:** Incorporating regular exercise, healthy nutrition, and adequate sleep.
- **Stress Reduction Practices:** Learning to set boundaries, prioritize tasks, and manage your workload effectively.

Think of long-term management as fortifying your home against future storms—these strategies make you stronger, more resilient, and better equipped to handle life's challenges.

The Foundation for the Rest of the Book

This chapter provides the groundwork for everything that follows. Anxiety is not a mysterious force beyond your control; it's a predictable process rooted in your body and mind. By understanding it, you've already taken the first step toward mastering it. The tools and techniques in the coming chapters will build on this foundation, empowering you to take back control—both in the moment and for the long term.

Turn the page, and let's start assembling your *Anxiety First Aid Kit*.

Chapter 2: Quick Calming Techniques for Immediate Relief

Anxiety can strike suddenly and without warning, leaving you feeling overwhelmed, disoriented, or trapped in a cycle of escalating fear. When this happens, having a toolkit of quick and effective techniques to calm your mind and body is invaluable. This chapter introduces proven methods you can use anywhere to regain control, reduce tension, and find a sense of calm in the moment. Each technique is simple, practical, and designed to work fast.

Breathing Exercises: The Power of Your Breath

Your breath is one of the most powerful tools for managing anxiety. By consciously controlling your breathing, you can send signals to your nervous system to calm down, counteracting the fight-or-flight response. Here are two highly effective techniques:

Box Breathing

Box breathing, also known as square breathing, is a simple but powerful method that promotes relaxation by focusing on equal intervals of inhaling, holding, exhaling, and holding again.

1. Sit comfortably and close your eyes if you're in a safe environment.
2. Inhale deeply through your nose for a count of **4 seconds**.
3. Hold your breath for **4 seconds**.
4. Exhale slowly through your mouth for **4 seconds**.
5. Hold your breath again for **4 seconds**.
6. Repeat the cycle 4-5 times or until you feel calmer.

Box breathing slows your heart rate and gives you a moment to reset, making it particularly useful in high-stress situations like meetings or public speaking.

4-7-8 Breathing

The 4-7-8 technique is designed to quickly calm the nervous system and promote a state of relaxation:

1. Inhale quietly through your nose for a count of **4 seconds**.
2. Hold your breath for **7 seconds**.
3. Exhale completely through your mouth for **8 seconds**, making a whooshing sound as you do.
4. Repeat the process for 4 cycles.

This method works because the extended exhale activates the parasympathetic nervous system, signaling your body to relax. It's especially effective before bed or when feeling panicked.

Grounding Techniques: Reconnecting to the Present

When anxiety takes over, it's easy to get lost in your thoughts. Grounding techniques bring you back to the present moment by focusing on your physical surroundings and senses.

The 5-4-3-2-1 Method

This popular grounding exercise uses your senses to anchor you in the here and now. Follow these steps:

1. **5 Things You Can See:** Look around and name five objects in your environment. It could be your phone, a tree, a picture on the wall—anything you can see.
2. **4 Things You Can Touch:** Pay attention to textures around you. Name four things you can physically feel, like the chair you're sitting on or the fabric of your clothes.
3. **3 Things You Can Hear:** Tune in to the sounds around you. It could be birds chirping, the hum of a refrigerator, or distant chatter.
4. **2 Things You Can Smell:** Identify two scents. If you can't smell anything immediate, think of scents you enjoy, like coffee or lavender.
5. **1 Thing You Can Taste:** Focus on a taste in your mouth, or imagine one you like (like mint gum or chocolate).

This method is effective because it forces your mind to shift away from anxious thoughts and focus on the tangible reality around you.

Sensory Tools: Engaging Your Senses

Sensory tools can help redirect your focus and soothe your body when anxiety feels overwhelming. These tools work by stimulating one or more of your senses—sight, touch, smell, taste, or hearing.

Stress Balls and Fidget Tools

Squeezing a stress ball or using a fidget spinner can channel anxious energy into a physical outlet. These tools are small, portable, and discreet, making them perfect for use in public or at work.

Aromatherapy

Certain scents have calming properties and can help reduce anxiety quickly. Examples include:

- **Lavender:** Known for its relaxing and sleep-promoting properties.
- **Peppermint:** Helps with mental clarity and refreshes the senses.
- **Chamomile:** Soothes tension and promotes relaxation.

Carry a small roller bottle of essential oil or a portable aromatherapy inhaler to use during moments of stress.

Weighted Objects

Weighted blankets or lap pads provide deep pressure stimulation, which can reduce anxiety and promote a sense of calm. If you're on the go, even holding a heavy object, like a water bottle, can have a grounding effect.

Quick Visualization Exercises: Escaping the Storm

Visualization exercises, also known as guided imagery, involve using your imagination to create calming mental images. These techniques are particularly effective for reducing anxiety in moments of overwhelm.

The Safe Place Visualization

1. Close your eyes and take a few deep breaths.
2. Imagine a place where you feel completely safe and at peace. This could be a beach, a forest, a cozy room, or anywhere that brings you comfort.
3. Engage your senses: Visualize the colors, hear the sounds, feel the textures, and even imagine the smells of this place.
4. Spend 2-5 minutes immersing yourself in this mental safe haven before gradually bringing your attention back to the present moment.

Cloud Watching

1. Picture a blue sky with fluffy white clouds floating by.
2. Imagine placing each anxious thought or feeling onto a cloud.
3. Watch the cloud drift away, taking the worry with it.
4. Repeat this process until you feel lighter and less burdened.

This exercise helps you detach from your anxiety, recognizing that thoughts and emotions are temporary and can "float away."

Putting It All Together

The techniques in this chapter are like the tools in a first aid kit—simple, effective, and ready to use in moments of need. You don't need to master all of them at once. Start with one or two methods that resonate with you and practice them regularly. Over time, these quick calming techniques will become second nature, allowing you to respond to anxiety with confidence and control.

Turn to this chapter whenever you need immediate relief. Whether it's a racing heart, spiraling thoughts, or an overwhelming sense of dread, these exercises are your lifeline back to calm.

Chapter 3: Building a Resilient Mindset

While quick-relief techniques are essential for calming anxiety in the moment, long-term resilience comes from cultivating a mindset that can weather life's challenges. Building a resilient mindset involves rewiring your thoughts, embracing mindfulness, and adopting practices that promote emotional stability and inner strength. This chapter will guide you through actionable strategies for transforming how you think and respond to anxiety.

The Power of Cognitive Reframing and Positive Self-Talk

Anxiety thrives on distorted thinking—those automatic, negative thoughts that often exaggerate or misinterpret reality. Cognitive reframing and positive self-talk are two powerful tools for taking control of your thought patterns.

What Is Cognitive Reframing?

Cognitive reframing is the process of identifying and challenging distorted thoughts, then replacing them with more balanced and constructive perspectives. Instead of viewing situations through a lens of fear or negativity, reframing allows you to see them objectively and even find opportunities for growth.

Steps to Cognitive Reframing:

1. **Identify the Thought:** Start by noticing the thought that's causing anxiety. For example, "I'm going to fail this presentation."

2. **Examine the Evidence:** Ask yourself, "What evidence supports this thought? What evidence contradicts it?" Often, you'll find that the fear is based more on assumption than fact.

3. **Reframe the Thought:** Replace the negative thought with a more balanced one. For example, "I've prepared thoroughly, and

I've done well in past presentations. Even if I make a mistake, I can recover."

4. **Practice Daily:** Reframing is a skill that improves with practice. Keep a journal to track your negative thoughts and your reframed responses.

What Is Positive Self-Talk?

Positive self-talk is the practice of speaking to yourself with kindness, encouragement, and optimism. It counteracts the inner critic that often amplifies anxiety.

Tips for Positive Self-Talk:

- Replace harsh judgments with affirmations. For example, change "I can't handle this" to "I've faced challenges before, and I can handle this too."
- Use your name or "you" in your self-talk for added impact, e.g., "You've got this, [Your Name]."
- Speak to yourself as you would to a close friend—compassionately and supportively.

Challenging and Replacing Anxious Thoughts

Anxious thoughts can feel automatic and overwhelming, but they are not unchangeable. By learning to challenge and replace these thoughts, you can regain control over your mental landscape.

The Thought-Challenging Process

1. **Catch the Thought:** Notice when you're experiencing an anxious thought. This requires mindfulness and self-awareness.
2. **Label the Thought:** Identify the type of cognitive distortion at play. Common distortions include:
   - **Catastrophizing:** Imagining the worst-case scenario.
   - **Black-and-White Thinking:** Seeing things as all good or all bad.
   - **Mind Reading:** Assuming you know what others are thinking.
3. **Ask Questions:** Challenge the validity of the thought:
   - Is this thought based on facts or assumptions?
   - What's the worst that could happen, and how likely is it?
   - How would I view this situation if I were calmer?
4. **Replace the Thought:** Develop a balanced alternative. For example:
   - Original thought: "I'm going to embarrass myself in front of everyone."
   - Balanced thought: "I might feel nervous, but I've prepared, and people will understand if I'm not perfect."

Mindfulness Practices for Daily Use

Mindfulness is the practice of staying present and fully engaged in the current moment. It's a cornerstone of anxiety management because it helps break the cycle of worry about the past or future.

Benefits of Mindfulness:

- Reduces overthinking and rumination.
- Improves emotional regulation.
- Enhances focus and clarity.

Simple Mindfulness Exercises:

1. **Mindful Breathing:** Spend 2-5 minutes focusing on your breath. Inhale slowly, notice the rise of your chest, and exhale fully. When your mind wanders, gently bring it back to your breath.
2. **Body Scan:** Take a few minutes to mentally scan your body from head to toe, noticing any tension or sensations without judgment.
3. **Mindful Eating:** Pay attention to the texture, taste, and aroma of your food. Eat slowly, savoring each bite, and avoid distractions like TV or phones.
4. **Five-Minute Mindfulness:** Set a timer for five minutes and observe your surroundings. Notice the sights, sounds, and sensations around you. Allow yourself to be fully present in the moment.

Integrate mindfulness into daily activities, like walking, cleaning, or even showering, by focusing fully on the task at hand.

The Role of Gratitude in Reducing Anxiety

Gratitude may seem like a simple concept, but its effects on anxiety can be profound. When you focus on what you're thankful for, it shifts your attention away from worries and negative thoughts, creating a more positive mental state.

How Gratitude Works:

- Activates areas of the brain associated with emotional regulation.
- Reduces stress hormones like cortisol.
- Encourages a sense of abundance and well-being.

Gratitude Practices:

1. **Gratitude Journaling:** Spend 5 minutes each day writing down 3-5 things you're grateful for. These can be as simple as "a sunny day" or as meaningful as "the support of a friend."
2. **Gratitude Reminders:** Set reminders on your phone to pause and think of one thing you're grateful for at that moment.
3. **Gratitude Visualization:** Close your eyes and visualize a person, place, or experience you're thankful for. Imagine the feelings of joy or peace it brings.

Practicing gratitude doesn't mean ignoring challenges or pretending life is perfect. It's about finding moments of light even in difficult times.

Cultivating Resilience: A Holistic Approach

Building a resilient mindset isn't about eliminating anxiety—it's about learning to navigate it with strength and grace. By mastering cognitive reframing, practicing mindfulness, and embracing gratitude, you create a mental foundation that allows you to face life's uncertainties with confidence.

This chapter's techniques are not one-time fixes; they are lifelong habits that grow stronger with practice. Start small, be patient with yourself, and remember: resilience is a journey, not a destination. With these tools, you are already well on your way to becoming the calm within your own storm.

Chapter 4: Physical Tools to Manage Anxiety

The mind and body are intricately connected, and anxiety doesn't just live in your thoughts—it also manifests physically. Addressing anxiety requires a holistic approach that includes taking care of your physical health. In this chapter, we'll explore the profound connection between physical and mental well-being, and provide actionable advice on how to use exercise, nutrition, hydration, and sleep to effectively manage anxiety.

The Connection Between Physical and Mental Health

Your body and mind are in constant communication, influencing each other in ways that are often subtle but significant. Poor physical health can exacerbate anxiety, while good physical habits can provide a strong foundation for mental resilience.

How the Body Affects the Mind

- **Hormonal Balance:** Physical health affects the production of hormones like cortisol (stress hormone) and serotonin (feel-good hormone), both of which play a key role in anxiety.
- **Nervous System Regulation:** Exercise, hydration, and sleep influence the autonomic nervous system, which controls your fight-or-flight response. Maintaining physical health helps keep this system balanced.
- **Energy Levels:** When your body is nourished and rested, you have more energy to cope with stress and manage your emotions.

How the Mind Affects the Body

Anxiety can trigger physical symptoms such as:

- Increased heart rate and blood pressure.
- Muscle tension and aches.
- Gastrointestinal discomfort (e.g., nausea, upset stomach). By addressing physical health, you can help reduce these symptoms and

create a positive feedback loop that benefits your mental well-being.

Exercise Routines to Reduce Anxiety

Exercise is one of the most effective physical tools for managing anxiety. It reduces stress hormones, increases endorphins (natural mood boosters), and promotes better sleep. The key is to find activities you enjoy and can commit to regularly.

Yoga for Anxiety Relief

Yoga combines movement, breath control, and mindfulness, making it an excellent tool for calming the mind and body.

- **Benefits:** Yoga helps reduce cortisol levels, increase flexibility, and improve overall relaxation.
- **Recommended Poses:**
  - **Child's Pose (Balasana):** Gently stretches the lower back and promotes relaxation.
  - **Cat-Cow Pose:** Loosens the spine and helps synchronize breath with movement.
  - **Legs-Up-the-Wall Pose:** Relieves tension in the lower body and promotes calm.
- **Frequency:** Practicing yoga 2-3 times a week for 20-30 minutes can significantly reduce anxiety symptoms.

Walking for Mental Clarity

Walking is a simple yet powerful form of exercise that requires no special equipment and can be done almost anywhere.

- **Benefits:** Walking boosts endorphins, reduces muscle tension, and provides a mental break.
- **Tips for Anxiety Relief:**
  - Walk in natural surroundings, like a park or trail, to benefit from the calming effects of nature.
  - Practice mindful walking by focusing on your breath, the sensation of your feet hitting the ground, and the sounds around you.
- **Frequency:** Aim for a 20-30 minute walk at least 4-5 times a week.

Other Activities to Consider

- **Swimming:** Provides a full-body workout and the soothing sensation of water.
- **Dancing:** Combines exercise with joy and self-expression.
- **Strength Training:** Builds physical resilience, which can translate to mental toughness.

The Role of Nutrition and Hydration in Anxiety Management

What you put into your body has a direct impact on your mental state. A balanced diet and proper hydration are essential for maintaining a calm and focused mind.

Nutrition Tips for Reducing Anxiety

1. **Eat Regularly:** Skipping meals can cause blood sugar levels to drop, leading to irritability and anxiety. Aim for balanced meals and healthy snacks throughout the day.
2. **Focus on Whole Foods:** Incorporate whole grains, lean proteins, fruits, vegetables, and healthy fats into your diet. Avoid processed foods high in sugar and refined carbohydrates, as they can cause energy crashes.
3. **Incorporate Omega-3s:** Foods rich in omega-3 fatty acids, like salmon, walnuts, and flaxseeds, support brain health and reduce inflammation linked to anxiety.
4. **Boost Magnesium Levels:** Magnesium-rich foods like spinach, almonds, and dark chocolate can help regulate the nervous system and reduce stress.
5. **Limit Stimulants:** Caffeine and alcohol can exacerbate anxiety. Opt for herbal teas or decaffeinated beverages instead.

Hydration: The Often-Overlooked Key

Dehydration can mimic or worsen anxiety symptoms, such as rapid heartbeat and dizziness.

- **How Much to Drink:** Aim for 8-10 glasses of water per day, or more if you're active or live in a hot climate.
- **Add Variety:** If plain water feels monotonous, try adding slices of lemon, cucumber, or mint for a refreshing twist.

Improving Sleep: A Cornerstone of Anxiety Management

Poor sleep and anxiety often feed into each other, creating a vicious cycle. Addressing sleep issues can significantly reduce anxiety and improve your overall quality of life.

Why Sleep Matters

- Sleep is when your brain processes emotions and resets for the next day. Without enough rest, anxiety can intensify.
- Lack of sleep affects the amygdala (emotional center of the brain), making it more reactive to stress.

Tips for Better Sleep

1. **Establish a Routine:** Go to bed and wake up at the same time every day, even on weekends. Consistency helps regulate your body's internal clock.
2. **Create a Sleep Sanctuary:** Make your bedroom a calm and inviting space. Use blackout curtains, keep the temperature cool, and minimize noise.
3. **Limit Screen Time:** Avoid screens (phones, tablets, TVs) at least an hour before bed. The blue light emitted by devices can disrupt your melatonin production.
4. **Practice Pre-Sleep Relaxation:**
   - Use breathing exercises or meditation to calm your mind.
   - Try progressive muscle relaxation: tense and release each muscle group from head to toe.
5. **Avoid Heavy Meals and Caffeine Before Bed:** Opt for a light snack if you're hungry, and avoid stimulants in the evening.

Sleep Aids and Supplements

- Consider natural aids like melatonin, valerian root, or chamomile tea, but consult with a healthcare professional before use.

Putting It All Together

Physical health is the foundation upon which mental resilience is built. By incorporating exercise, proper nutrition, hydration, and healthy sleep habits into your routine, you can create a body that supports a calm and focused mind. These tools are not just about reducing anxiety—they're about empowering you to take control of your overall well-being.

Start small by choosing one or two areas to focus on, then gradually integrate the others into your life. Over time, you'll find that these physical practices become second nature, helping you navigate life with greater ease and confidence.

Chapter 5: Creating Your Personal Anxiety First Aid Kit

Anxiety can feel overwhelming and unpredictable, but having a personalized toolkit of relief strategies can empower you to take control when it strikes. Just like a physical first aid kit contains supplies to treat injuries, your anxiety first aid kit will contain tools tailored to your unique needs—tools that help calm your mind, ground your body, and restore your sense of balance. In this chapter, we'll guide you through creating your own anxiety first aid kit, complete with physical items, mental resources, and actionable techniques.

Why You Need an Anxiety First Aid Kit

Anxiety doesn't always announce its arrival. It can show up unexpectedly—during a meeting, on a crowded bus, or in the middle of the night. When it does, having a pre-prepared toolkit allows you to respond immediately and effectively.

Your anxiety first aid kit serves several purposes:

1. **Quick Access to Tools:** Having everything in one place saves you the stress of searching for relief strategies in the moment.
2. **Sense of Control:** The act of building and using your kit reinforces that anxiety is manageable.
3. **Personalized Support:** Your kit reflects your unique preferences and coping mechanisms, making it more effective.

What to Include in Your Anxiety First Aid Kit

Your anxiety toolkit should contain a mix of physical items, mental resources, and techniques that work for you. Below are some suggestions to get started:

1. Affirmation Cards

Affirmation cards are small, portable reminders of your inner strength and resilience. They can help shift your mindset during moments of anxiety.

- Examples of affirmations:
    - "This feeling is temporary, and I can handle it."
    - "I am safe and capable of overcoming this moment."
    - "I have the tools I need to find calm."
- **How to Use Them:** Write affirmations on index cards or purchase pre-made ones. Keep them in your bag, wallet, or desk.

2. Sensory Tools

Engaging your senses is a powerful way to ground yourself and interrupt anxious thoughts.

- **Suggestions:**
    - Stress balls or fidget toys for tactile stimulation.
    - Aromatherapy items like lavender-scented sachets or roll-on essential oils.
    - A small, soft object (e.g., a piece of fabric or a smooth stone) to hold and touch.
- **How to Use Them:** Select sensory tools that you find soothing and keep them in an accessible place, like your desk or car.

3. Calming Playlists

Music has a direct impact on your mood and nervous system. Create playlists that help you relax or boost your mood.

- **Suggestions:**
    - Soft instrumental music or nature sounds for relaxation.
    - Upbeat tracks to lift your energy and focus.
    - Guided meditations or calming podcasts for moments of deep stress.
- **How to Use Them:** Save playlists to your phone so they're accessible even offline.

4. Favorite Grounding Techniques

Grounding techniques are essential for regaining a sense of control during anxious moments.

- **Suggestions:**
    - The 5-4-3-2-1 Method (described in Chapter 2).
    - Deep breathing exercises like 4-7-8 breathing.
    - Visualization exercises, such as imagining a safe place.
- **How to Use Them:** Write down a list of your go-to techniques and keep it in your kit for reference.

5. Physical Comfort Items

Small, comforting items can help you feel secure during times of stress.

- **Suggestions:**
    - A cozy scarf, blanket, or sweater.
    - Herbal tea bags for a warm, soothing drink.
    - A reusable water bottle to stay hydrated.
- **How to Use Them:** Keep these items in your home or workspace for easy access.

6. Written Resources

Sometimes, reading calming or inspirational words can help you shift your focus.

- **Suggestions:**
    - A small journal for jotting down thoughts or feelings.
    - A book of poetry, short stories, or calming essays.
    - Anxiety-related worksheets, such as cognitive reframing prompts.
- **How to Use Them:** Include these items for moments when you need quiet reflection or a mental distraction.

Checklist for Building Your Toolkit

Below is a step-by-step checklist to help you compile your personal anxiety first aid kit. Remember, this is a starting point—you can customize it to suit your preferences.

1. **Physical Items:**
   - Stress ball or fidget toy.
   - Aromatherapy item (e.g., lavender oil).
   - Soft object (e.g., fabric, smooth stone).
   - Water bottle and herbal tea bags.
   - Comfort item (e.g., scarf, blanket).

2. **Digital Resources:**
   - Calming music playlist.
   - Guided meditation or mindfulness app.
   - Affirmation list saved on your phone.

3. **Mental Techniques:**
   - Written list of grounding exercises.
   - Breathing techniques (e.g., box breathing).
   - Visualization instructions for your safe space.

4. **Written Materials:**
   - Affirmation cards or positive quotes.
   - Anxiety-related worksheets or prompts.
   - Journal or notebook for writing.

5. **Custom Items:**
   - Any additional items that bring you comfort or calm.

Adapting Your Toolkit as Your Needs Change

Your anxiety first aid kit is not a static tool; it should evolve as your needs and preferences change. Here's how to keep it relevant:

1. **Review Regularly:** Set aside time every few months to assess what's working and what's not. Remove items you no longer use and add new ones.
2. **Experiment:** Try new techniques or tools you come across and see if they resonate with you.
3. **Adapt to Different Environments:** Create mini versions of your toolkit for work, travel, or other specific settings.
4. **Listen to Yourself:** Your anxiety patterns may shift over time. Stay attuned to what helps you most in different situations.

A Kit That Reflects You

Your anxiety first aid kit is more than just a collection of tools—it's a reflection of your commitment to self-care and emotional well-being. It's a resource you can turn to whenever anxiety strikes, offering comfort, relief, and empowerment.

Remember, there's no right or wrong way to build your kit. Start with the suggestions in this chapter, personalize them to suit your needs, and adapt as you grow. Over time, you'll find that this simple yet powerful resource becomes an invaluable part of your life.

With your personalized toolkit in hand, you are equipped to face the challenges of anxiety with resilience and confidence. Let this be your reminder: you have the tools to calm the storm, and the strength to find peace within it.

Appendix A: Additional Resources

Managing anxiety is a journey, and having access to a wide range of tools and support systems can make all the difference. This appendix provides a curated list of resources—books, apps, websites, and support groups—that can deepen your understanding of anxiety and enhance your coping strategies. Whether you're looking for self-help, professional guidance, or community support, this list offers a variety of options to explore.

Books on Anxiety Management

These books provide valuable insights and practical tools for understanding and managing anxiety.

1. **"The Anxiety and Phobia Workbook" by Edmund J. Bourne, PhD**

   A comprehensive workbook with exercises and strategies for overcoming anxiety and phobias.

2. **"Dare: The New Way to End Anxiety and Stop Panic Attacks" by Barry McDonagh**

   A fresh approach to tackling anxiety by facing fears and building resilience.

3. **"Rewire Your Anxious Brain" by Catherine M. Pittman, PhD, and Elizabeth M. Karle, MLIS**

   Explores the neuroscience behind anxiety and offers actionable steps to change thought patterns.

4. **"The Worry Trick: How Your Brain Tricks You into Expecting the Worst and What You Can Do About It" by David A. Carbonell, PhD**

   Practical advice on breaking free from chronic worry and anxiety loops.

5. **"Self-Compassion: The Proven Power of Being Kind to Yourself" by Kristin Neff, PhD**
   Focuses on the importance of self-kindness in managing anxiety and building emotional resilience.

Apps for Anxiety Relief

Technology can be a powerful ally in managing anxiety. These apps provide guided meditations, mindfulness exercises, and tracking tools to help you stay grounded:

1. **Calm**
   - Offers guided meditations, breathing exercises, and soothing soundscapes.
   - Available on iOS and Android.
2. **Headspace**
   - A popular app for learning mindfulness and meditation, with programs specifically for stress and anxiety.
   - Available on iOS and Android.
3. **Sanvello**
   - Combines cognitive-behavioral therapy (CBT), mindfulness, and mood tracking.
   - Available on iOS and Android.
4. **Breethe**
   - Focuses on stress reduction with meditations, sleep aids, and motivational talks.
   - Available on iOS and Android.
5. **MindShift CBT**
   - Provides CBT-based tools for challenging anxious thoughts and behaviors.
   - Available on iOS and Android.

Websites for Anxiety Management

Explore these websites for expert advice, self-help resources, and community support:

1. **Anxiety and Depression Association of America (ADAA)**
   - Website: www.adaa.org
   - Offers educational resources, webinars, and a therapist directory.
2. **HelpGuide**
   - Website: www.helpguide.org
   - Provides in-depth articles on anxiety, stress management, and mental health.
3. **National Institute of Mental Health (NIMH)**
   - Website: www.nimh.nih.gov
   - A reliable source for research-based information on anxiety disorders.
4. **Calm Clinic**
   - Website: www.calmclinic.com
   - Focuses on understanding anxiety symptoms and provides coping techniques.
5. **Verywell Mind**
   - Website: www.verywellmind.com
   - Features expert advice on mental health topics, including anxiety management.

Meditation and Mindfulness Resources

Meditation and mindfulness are powerful tools for reducing anxiety. Here are some trusted resources to help you get started:

1. **Insight Timer**
    - Website: www.insighttimer.com
    - A free app and website offering thousands of guided meditations for anxiety, sleep, and stress.
2. **Tara Brach's Free Guided Meditations**
    - Website: www.tarabrach.com/meditation
    - A collection of free meditations led by renowned mindfulness teacher Tara Brach.
3. **Mindful.org**
    - Website: www.mindful.org
    - Articles, tips, and guided practices for incorporating mindfulness into daily life.
4. **The Honest Guys YouTube Channel**
    - Website: www.youtube.com/thehonestguys
    - Relaxing guided meditations and visualization exercises for anxiety relief.
5. **Jon Kabat-Zinn's Guided Mindfulness Practices**
    - Available for purchase or streaming. Kabat-Zinn is a pioneer in mindfulness-based stress reduction (MBSR).

Mental Health Hotlines and Support Groups

If you're experiencing severe anxiety or need someone to talk to, these hotlines and support groups can provide immediate help:

Hotlines (U.S.):

1. **National Suicide Prevention Lifeline**
    - Phone: 988 or 1-800-273-TALK (1-800-273-8255)
    - Website: www.suicidepreventionlifeline.org
    - Offers 24/7 support for those in crisis.
2. **SAMHSA's National Helpline**
    - Phone: 1-800-662-HELP (1-800-662-4357)
    - Website: www.samhsa.gov/find-help/national-helpline
    - A confidential, 24/7 helpline for substance abuse and mental health services.
3. **Crisis Text Line**
    - Text HOME to 741741
    - Website: www.crisistextline.org
    - Provides free, 24/7 text support for any mental health crisis.
4. **The Trevor Project (LGBTQ+ Support)**
    - Phone: 1-866-488-7386
    - Text START to 678678
    - Website: www.thetrevorproject.org

International Hotlines:

- Visit www.befrienders.org for a directory of international mental health hotlines.

Support Groups:

1. **Anxiety and Depression Support Groups (ADAA)**
   - Website: www.adaa.org/supportgroups
   - Find online or local support groups for anxiety and depression.
2. **Mental Health America (MHA)**
   - Website: www.mhanational.org/find-support-groups
   - Offers a directory of support groups for various mental health challenges.
3. **NAMI Connection Recovery Support Groups**
   - Website: www.nami.org
   - Free peer-led support groups for people with mental health conditions.
4. **Meetup**
   - Website: www.meetup.com
   - Search for local or virtual anxiety support groups in your area.

Closing Thoughts

This appendix is a gateway to deeper exploration and additional support. Whether you're seeking self-help strategies, professional advice, or community connection, these resources are here to empower you on your journey to managing anxiety. Bookmark this section or save it for future reference as your needs evolve. You're not alone, and help is always within reach.

Appendix B: Worksheets and Checklists

This appendix provides practical tools to help you implement the strategies discussed in the book. From tracking your anxiety to maintaining a self-care routine and practicing calming techniques, these worksheets and checklists are designed to make managing anxiety more structured and actionable. Feel free to print or copy these resources for daily use.

1. Anxiety Tracking Sheet

Use this sheet to identify patterns and triggers in your anxiety. By tracking your experiences, you can gain insights into what causes your anxiety and develop strategies to address it.

Date	Time	Situation/ Trigger	Physical Symptoms	Emotions/ Thoughts	Coping Strategy Used	Effectiveness (1-5)
YYYY-MM-DD	HH:MM	E.g., work deadline, crowded space	Racing heart, sweating, dizziness	Fear, "I can't handle this"	Box breathing, 5-4-3-2-1 grounding	4
YYYY-MM-DD	HH:MM					

Instructions:

1. Fill in the date and time when you feel anxious.
2. Describe the situation or trigger (e.g., a specific event, thought, or place).
3. List the physical symptoms you experienced (e.g., racing heart, sweating).
4. Write down the emotions or thoughts you had during the episode.
5. Note the coping strategy you used to manage the anxiety (e.g., breathing exercises, visualization).
6. Rate the effectiveness of the strategy on a scale of 1 (not effective) to 5 (very effective).

Review your entries weekly to identify recurring triggers and refine your coping strategies.

2. Daily Self-Care Checklist

Maintaining mental health requires consistent self-care. This checklist helps you build a routine that supports your well-being.

Self-Care Activity	Completed? (✓)
Morning Routine	
Drink a glass of water first thing.	
Spend 5 minutes practicing mindfulness or breathing exercises.	
Eat a healthy breakfast.	
Work/Daytime Routine	
Take regular breaks (every 1-2 hours) to stretch or walk.	
Practice the 5-4-3-2-1 grounding technique if feeling stressed.	
Stay hydrated (aim for 8-10 glasses of water).	
Eat a balanced lunch with whole foods.	
Evening Routine	
Reflect on three things you're grateful for today.	

Self-Care Activity	Completed? (✓)
Limit screen time at least 1 hour before bed.	
Do a relaxing activity (e.g., reading, journaling).	
Practice a calming bedtime routine (e.g., warm shower, dim lights).	
Physical Care	
Exercise or move your body for at least 20 minutes.	
Eat three balanced meals and healthy snacks.	
Get 7-9 hours of sleep.	
Emotional and Mental Care	
Spend time on a hobby or creative activity.	
Connect with a friend or loved one.	
Journal or reflect on your emotions.	
Practice positive self-talk or affirmations.	

Instructions:

- Place a checkmark (✓) next to each completed activity.
- Use this checklist daily to track your self-care habits and identify areas for improvement.

3. Step-by-Step Guides for Chapter 2 Techniques

The techniques in Chapter 2 are designed for immediate relief. These step-by-step guides will make it easy to practice and remember them when needed.

Box Breathing

1. Sit comfortably and close your eyes if possible.
2. Inhale deeply through your nose for **4 seconds**.
3. Hold your breath for **4 seconds**.
4. Exhale slowly through your mouth for **4 seconds**.
5. Hold your breath again for **4 seconds**.
6. Repeat the cycle 4-5 times or until you feel calmer.

4-7-8 Breathing

1. Inhale quietly through your nose for **4 seconds**.
2. Hold your breath for **7 seconds**.
3. Exhale completely through your mouth for **8 seconds**, making a soft whooshing sound.
4. Repeat the process 4 times.

5-4-3-2-1 Grounding Technique

1. **5 Things You Can See:** Look around and name five things you can see.
2. **4 Things You Can Touch:** Name four things you can physically feel.
3. **3 Things You Can Hear:** Identify three sounds in your environment.
4. **2 Things You Can Smell:** Focus on two scents (or imagine smells if none are present).
5. **1 Thing You Can Taste:** Identify one taste in your mouth or think of a favorite taste.

Safe Place Visualization

1. Close your eyes and take a deep breath.
2. Imagine a place where you feel completely safe and relaxed.
3. Engage your senses—what do you see, hear, smell, and feel in this place?
4. Spend 2-5 minutes immersing yourself in this mental sanctuary.

How to Use This Appendix

These worksheets and checklists are meant to be practical, adaptable tools.

- **Keep Copies Handy:** Print or save multiple copies of the anxiety tracking sheet and self-care checklist for regular use.
- **Customize as Needed:** Modify the resources to suit your specific needs and preferences.

- **Review Regularly:** Set aside time to review your completed sheets and identify patterns, triggers, and effective strategies.

By integrating these tools into your routine, you'll develop a deeper understanding of your anxiety and the strategies that work best for you. Over time, these practices will help you build resilience and maintain a balanced, calm state of mind.

<u>Message from the Author:</u>

I hope you enjoyed this book, I love astrology and knew there was not a book such as this out on the shelf. I love metaphysical items as well. Please check out my other books:

-Life of Government Benefits

-My life of Hell

-My life with Hydrocephalus

-Red Sky

-World Domination:Woman's rule

-World Domination:Woman's Rule 2: The War

-Life and Banishment of Apophis: book 1

-The Kidney Friendly Diet

-The Ultimate Hemp Cookbook

-Creating a Dispensary(legally)

-Cleanliness throughout life: the importance of showering from childhood to adulthood.

-Strong Roots: The Risks of Overcoddling children

-Hemp Horoscopes: Cosmic Insights and Earthly Healing

- Celestial Hemp Navigating the Zodiac: Through the Green Cosmos

-Astrological Hemp: Aligning The Stars with Earth's Ancient Herb

-The Astrological Guide to Hemp: Stars, Signs, and Sacred Leaves

-Green Growth: Innovative Marketing Strategies for your Hemp Products and Dispensary

-Cosmic Cannabis

-Astrological Munchies

-Henry The Hemp

-Zodiacal Roots: The Astrological Soul Of Hemp

- **Green Constellations: Intersection of Hemp and Zodiac**

-Hemp in The Houses: An astrological Adventure Through The Cannabis Galaxy

-Galactic Ganja Guide

Heavenly Hemp

Zodiac Leaves

Doctor Who Astrology

Cannastrology

Stellar Satvias and Cosmic Indicas

<u>Celestial Cannabis: A Zodiac Journey</u>

AstroHerbology: The Sky and The Soil: Volume 1

AstroHerbology:Celestial Cannabis:Volume 2

Cosmic Cannabis Cultivation

The Starry Guide to Herbal Harmony: Volume 1

The Starry Guide to Herbal Harmony: Cannabis Universe: Volume 2

Yugioh Astrology: Astrological Guide to Deck, Duels and more

Nightmare Mansion: Echoes of The Abyss

Nightmare Mansion 2: Legacy of Shadows

Nightmare Mansion 3: Shadows of the Forgotten

Nightmare Mansion 4: Echoes of the Damned

The Life and Banishment of Apophis: Book 2

Nightmare Mansion: Halls of Despair

<u>Healing with Herb: Cannabis and Hydrocephalus</u>

<u>Planetary Pot: Aligning with Astrological Herbs: Volume 1</u>

Fast Track to Freedom: 30 Days to Financial Independence Using AI, Assets, and Agile Hustles

<u>Cosmic Hemp Pathways</u>

How to Become Financially Free in 30 Days: 10,000 Paths to Prosperity

Zodiacal Herbage: Astrological Insights: Volume 1

Nightmare Mansion: Whispers in the Walls

The Daleks Invade Atlantis

Henry the hemp and Hydrocephalus

10X The Kidney Friendly Diet

Cannabis Universe: Adult coloring book

Hemp Astrology: The Healing Power of the Stars

Zodiacal Herbage: Astrological Insights: Cannabis Universe: Volume 2

<u>Planetary Pot: Aligning with Astrological Herbs: Cannabis Universes: Volume 2</u>

Doctor Who Meets the Replicators and SG-1: The Ultimate Battle for Survival

Nightmare Mansion: Curse of the Blood Moon

<u>The Celestial Stoner: A Guide to the Zodiac</u>

Cosmic Pleasures: Sex Toy Astrology for Every Sign

Hydrocephalus Astrology: Navigating the Stars and Healing Waters

Lapis and the Mischievous Chocolate Bar

Celestial Positions: Sexual Astrology for Every Sign

Apophis's Shadow Work Journal: **:** A Journey of Self-Discovery and Healing

Kinky Cosmos: Sexual Kink Astrology for Every Sign

Digital Cosmos: The Astrological Digimon Compendium

Stellar Seeds: The Cosmic Guide to Growing with Astrology

Apophis's Daily Gratitude Journal

Cat Astrology: Feline Mysteries of the Cosmos

The Cosmic Kama Sutra: An Astrological Guide to Sexual Positions

Unleash Your Potential: A Guided Journal Powered by AI Insights

Whispers of the Enchanted Grove

Cosmic Pleasures: An Astrological Guide to Sexual Kinks

369, 12 Manifestation Journal

Whisper of the nocturne journal(blank journal for writing or drawing)

The Boogey Book

Locked In Reflection: A Chastity Journey Through Locktober

Generating Wealth Quickly:

How to Generate $100,000 in 24 Hours

Star Magic: Harness the Power of the Universe

The Flatulence Chronicles: A Fart Journal for Self-Discovery

The Doctor and The Death Moth

Seize the Day: A Personal Seizure Tracking Journal

The Ultimate Boogeyman Safari: A Journey into the Boogie World and Beyond

Whispers of Samhain: 1,000 Spells of Love, Luck, and Lunar Magic: Samhain Spell Book

Apophis's guides:

Witch's Spellbook Crafting Guide for Halloween

<u>Frost & Flame: The Enchanted Yule Grimoire of 1000 Winter Spells</u>

<u>The Ultimate Boogey Goo Guide & Spooky Activities for Halloween Fun</u>

Harmony of the Scales: A Libra's Spellcraft for Balance and Beauty

The Enchanted Advent: 36 Days of Christmas Wonders

Nightmare Mansion: The Labyrinth of Screams

Harvest of Enchantment: 1,000 Spells of Gratitude, Love, and Fortune for Thanksgiving

The Boogey Chronicles: A Journal of Nightly Encounters and Shadowy Secrets

The 12 Days of Financial Freedom: A Step-by-Step Christmas Countdown to Transform Your Finances

Sigil of the Eternal Spiral Blank Journal

A Christmas Feast: Timeless Recipes for Every Meal

Holiday Stress-Free Solutions: A Survival Guide to Thriving During the Festive Season

Yu-Gi-Oh! Holiday Gifting Mastery: The Ultimate Guide for Fans and Newcomers Alike

Holiday Harmony: A Hydrocephalus Survival Guide for the Festive Season

Celestial Craft: The Witch's Almanac for 2025 – A Cosmic Guide to Manifestations, Moons, and Mystical Events

Doctor Who: The Toymaker's Winter Wonderland

Tulsa King Unveiled: A Thrilling Guide to Stallone's Mafia Masterpiece

Pendulum Craft: A Complete Guide to Crafting and Using Personalized Divination Tools

Nightmare Mansion: Santa's Eternal Eve

Starlight Noel: A Cosmic Journey through Christmas Mysteries

The Dark Architect: Unlocking the Blueprint of Existence

Surviving the Embrace: The Ultimate Guide to Encounters with The Hugging Molly

The Enchanted Codex: Secrets of the Craft for Witches, Wiccans, and Pagans

Harvest of Gratitude: A Complete Thanksgiving Guide

Yuletide Essentials: A Complete Guide to an Authentic and Magical Christmas

Celestial Smokes: A Cosmic Guide to Cigars and Astrology

Living in Balance: A Comprehensive Survival Guide to Thriving with Diabetes Insipidus

Cosmic Symbiosis: The Venom Zodiac Chronicles

The Cursed Paw of Ambition

Cosmic Symbiosis: The Astrological Venom Journal

Celestial Wonders Unfold: A Stargazer's Guide to the Cosmos (2024-2029)

The Ultimate Black Friday Prepper's Guide: Mastering Shopping Strategies and Savings

Cosmic Sales: The Astrological Guide to Black Friday Shopping

Legends of the Corn Mother and Other Harvest Myths

Whispers of the Harvest: The Corn Mother's Journal

The Evergreen Spellbook

The Doctor Meets the Boogeyman

The White Witch of Rose Hall's SpellBook

The Gingerbread Golem's Shadow: A Study in Sweet Darkness

The Gingerbread Golem Codex: An Academic Exploration of Sweet Myths

The Gingerbread Golem Grimoire: Sweet Magicks and Spells for the Festive Witch

The Curse of the Gingerbread Golem

10-minute Christmas Crafts for kids

<u>Christmas Crisis Solutions: The Ultimate Last-Minute Survival Guide</u>

Gingerbread Golem Recipes: Holiday Treats with a Magical Twist

The Infinite Key: Unlocking Mystical Secrets of the Ages

Enchanted Yule: A Wiccan and Pagan Guide to a Magical and Memorable Season

Dinosaurs of Power: Unlocking Ancient Magick

Astro-Dinos: The Cosmic Guide to Prehistoric Wisdom

Gallifrey's Yule Logs: A Festive Doctor Who Cookbook

The Dino Grimoire: Secrets of Prehistoric Magick

The Gift They Never Knew They Needed

The Gingerbread Golem's Culinary Alchemy: Enchanting Recipes for a Sweetly Dark Feast

A Time Lord Christmas: Holiday Adventures with the Doctor

Krampusproofing Your Home: Defensive Strategies for Yule

Silent Frights: A Collection of Christmas Creepypastas to Chill Your Bones

Santa Raptor's Jolly Carnage: A Dino-Claus Christmas Tale

Prehistoric Palettes: A Dino Wicca Coloring Journey

The Christmas Wishkeeper Chronicles

The Starlight Sleigh: A Holiday Journey
Elf Secrets: The True Magic of the North Pole
Candy Cane Conjurations
Cooking with Kids: Recipes Under 20 Minutes
Doctor Who: The TARDIS Confiscation
If you want solar for your home go here: https://www.harborsolar.live/apophisenterprises/

Get Some Tarot cards: https://www.makeplayingcards.com/sell/ apophis-occult-shop

Get   some   shirts: https://www.bonfire.com/store/apophis-shirt-emporium/

Instagrams:
@apophis_enterprises,
@apophisbookemporium,
@apophisscardshop
Twitter: @apophisenterpr1
 Tiktok:@apophisenterprise
Youtube: @sg1fan23477, @FiresideRetreatKingdom
Hive: @sg1fan23477
CheeLee: @SG1fan23477

Podcast: Apophis Chat Zone: https://open.spotify.com/show/
5zXbrCLEV2xzCp8ybrfHsk?si=fb4d4fdbdce44dec

Newsletter: https://apophiss-newsletter-27c897.beehiiv.com/

If you want to support me or see posts of other projects that I have come over to: **<u>buymeacoffee.com/mpetchinskg</u>**

I post there daily several times a day

Get your Dinowicca or Christmas themed digital products, especially Santa Raptor songs and other musics. Here: **https://sg1fan23477.gumroad.com**

Apophis Yuletide Digital has not only digital Christmas items, but it will have all things with Dinowicca as well as other Digital products.